Say Something

arranged for harp by Sylvia Woods

Words and Music by
Ian Axel, Chad Vaccarino
and Mike Campbell

This music features a pedal point (also called a pedal note or pedal tone), which is a sustained or continually repeated note that is held constant while harmonies change in other parts.

A pedal point is usually found in the bass, but here it is in the middle register. Virtually every measure includes a middle C note on the downbeat. Sometimes it is played with the right hand, and at other times with the left. But it is almost always there.

This pedal point harmony is what originally drew me into this beautiful piece of music the first time I heard it on the radio.

The harp range required for this piece is 24 strings from a low C up to an E. It can be played on 24-string to 26-string harps with a C as the lowest string if you play both hands an octave higher than written.

No sharping levers are required to play this piece.

I hope you enjoy playing this arrangement on the harp.

Sylvia Woods

Say Something

Words and Music by Ian Axel,
Chad Vaccarino and Mike Campbell
Harp Arrangement by Sylvia Woods

Moderately

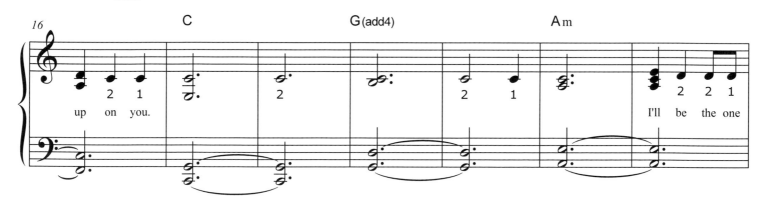

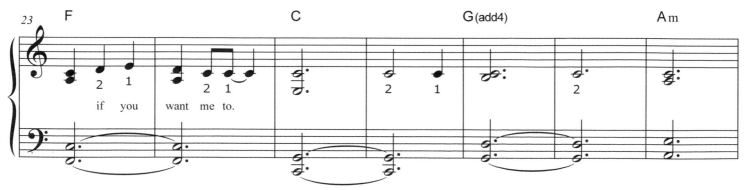

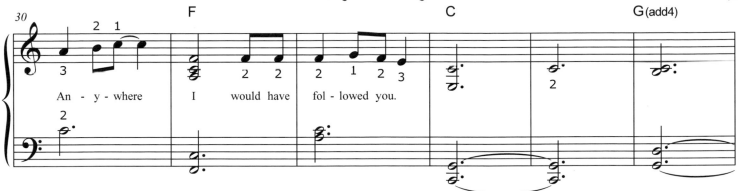

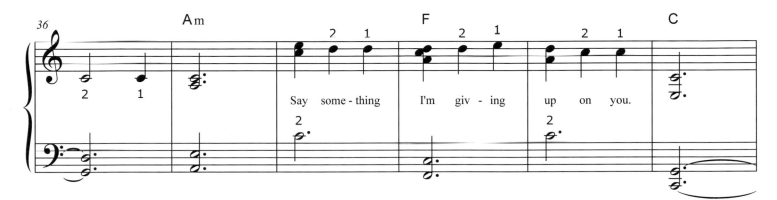

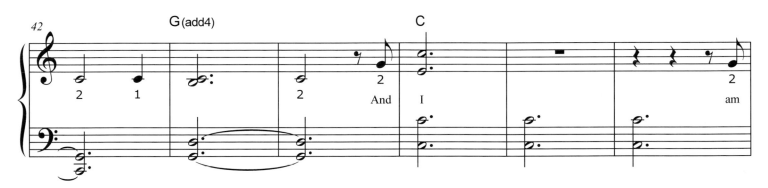

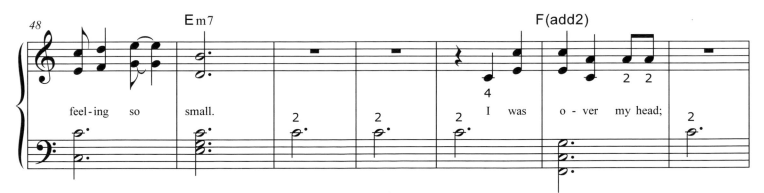

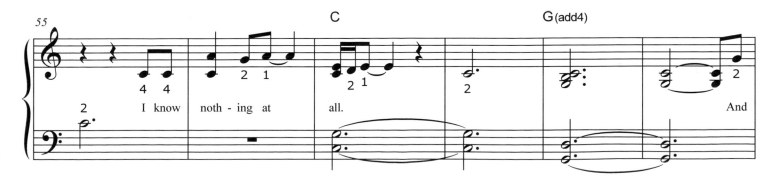

I   will   stum - ble   and   fall.
I   will   swal - low   my   pride.

I'm still   learn - ing   to   love,   just   start - ing   to   crawl.
You're the   one   that   I   love,   and I'm   say - ing good - bye.

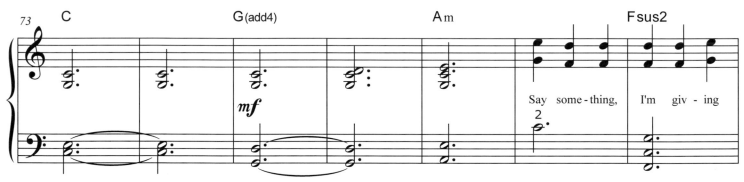

Say some - thing,   I'm   giv - ing

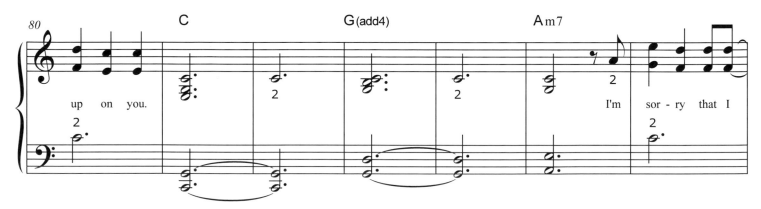

up on you.   I'm   sor - ry that I

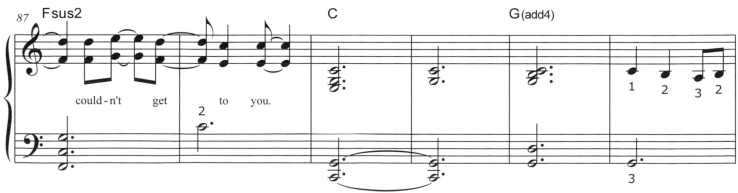

could - n't   get   to   you.